TAMBOURINES!
TAMBOURINES
TO GLORY!

TAMBOURINES!
TAMBOURINES
TO GLORY!

Prayers and Poems

SELECTED BY NANCY LARRICK

Illustrated by Geri Greinke

THE WESTMINSTER PRESS
Philadelphia

BOOK DESIGN BY DOROTHY ALDEN SMITH

For Acknowledgments, see pp. 103–106.

First edition

Published by The Westminster Press®
Philadelphia, Pennsylvania

PRINTED IN THE UNITED STATES OF AMERICA
9 8 7 6 5 4 3 2 1

Library of Congress Cataloging in Publication Data

Main entry under title

Tambourines! Tambourines to glory!

Includes indexes.
SUMMARY: A collection of short prayers on many subjects, from various sources in poetry and folklore
1. Children—Prayer-books and devotions—English [1. Prayers. 2. Religions—Poetry] I. Larrick, Nancy. II. Greinke, Geri, ill.
BV4870.T27   242'.82   81-23158
ISBN 0-664-32689-7   AACR2

CONTENTS

THE PRAYERS OF CHILDHOOD

Childhood is a time for reaching out, for trying new experiences and exploring new ideas. It is a time for reaching up, too, following the lead of those who are older and wiser.

In these impressionable years, children learn of a higher power bringing peace and strength to all humanity. As they hear the simple prayers of childhood and learn to voice their own petitions, children are building a personal connection that may flower into an abiding friendship with the one they call God, Father, or simply Great Spirit.

Peoples of all nations and all religions seem to have prayers which children understand and respond to. From these I have selected seventy-six for this little book.

They are in the simple, conversational language that children use comfortably and happily. Many are in the words of the children, sometimes about the events and difficulties of their days.

Some are prayers attributed to animals—for example, "The Prayer of the Monkey" and "The Prayer of the Little Ducks"—but these are so personal that each seems to be the prayer of a child.

Along with the prayers that are clearly for the very young, I have included those with special appeal to older children: a prayer for the safe flight of a pilot, a prayer of protest from coal miners, and an Israeli girl's prayer for peace, among others.

Selections have been taken from many sources: St. Francis of Assisi, American Indian tribes, Bushmen of southern Africa, the Breton fishermen, Ogden Nash, Mary Baker Eddy, and a host of poets, known and unknown.

Despite their diversity, a strong unifying theme sings out in these prayers of many nations and many religions. All reveal a heartwarming faith in a divine being who hears the prayers of a vast comradeship.

Tambourines! Tambourines to glory!

—NANCY LARRICK

GET OUT YOUR
RAINBOW COLORS

SEND US A RAINBOW

You, whose day it is,
Make it beautiful.
Get out your rainbow colors,
So it will be beautiful.

From the Nootka
Indians of North America

11

MORNING

Dear Lord my God,
Good morning!

The rain is falling
to wake the wintry world,
to green the grass,
to bring blossoms to the tree
　　outside my window.

The world and I wake up for you.
Alleluia!

Madeleine L'Engle

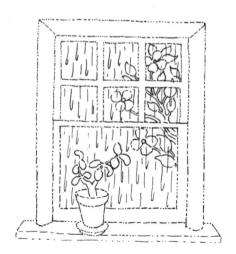

THANK YOU

Thank you, Sun, for being here!
Thank you, Stream, for being near!
Thank you, Flowers!
Thank you, Summer Showers!

13

Lily Breek
Age 6

PRAYER

Thank you for the sun,
      the sky,
   for all the things that like to fly,
      the shining rain that turns grass green,
      the earth we know—
      the world unseen—
  for stars and night, and once again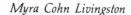
      the every morning sun. Amen.

Myra Cohn Livingston

14

NIGHT

Tonight the earth
is crowned with stars,
a soft wind hums a tune,
And for a hat
the pine tree wears
a slice of saucy moon,
Good night, World!
Good night, God!

15

Catherine and Peter Marshall

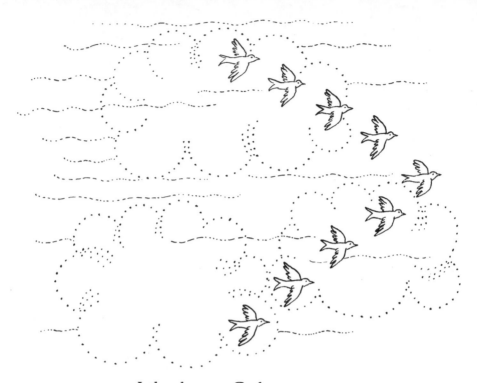

I thank you, God,
That swallows know their way
In the great sky;
That grass, all brown today,
And dead and dry,
Will quiver in the sun
All green and gay
When Winter's done.

16

Louise Driscoll
From "Thanksgiving"

WHITE FLOATING CLOUDS

White floating clouds,
Clouds like the plains,
Come and water the earth.
Sun, embrace the earth
that she may be fruitful.
Moon, lion of the north,
Bear of the west,
Badger of the south,
Wolf of the east,
Eagle of the heavens,
Shrew of the earth,
Elder war hero,
Warriors of the six mountains of the world,
Intercede with the cloud people for us
That they may water the earth.

From the Sia
Indians of the Southwest

Cover my earth mother four times with many flowers.
Let the heavens be covered with the banked-up clouds.
Let the earth be covered with fog;
    cover the earth with rains.
Great waters, rains, cover the earth.
Lightning cover the earth.
Let thunder be heard over the earth;
    let thunder be heard;
Let thunder be heard over the six regions of the earth.

From the Zuñi
Indians of the Southwest
From "Invocation to the U'wannami, Part III"

18

A PRAYER IN SPRING

Oh, give us pleasure in the flowers today;
And give us not to think so far away
As the uncertain harvest; keep us here
All simply in the springing of the year.

Oh, give us pleasure in the orchard white,
Like nothing else by day, like ghosts by night;
And make us happy in the happy bees,
The swarm dilating round the perfect trees.

And make us happy in the darting bird
That suddenly above the bees is heard,
The meteor that thrusts in with needle bill,
And off a blossom in mid air stands still.

For this is love and nothing else is love,
The which it is reserved for God above
To sanctify to what far ends He will,
But which it only needs that we fulfill.

Robert Frost

i thank You God for most this amazing
day:for the leaping greenly spirits of trees
and a blue true dream of sky;and for everything
which is natural which is infinite which is yes

(i who have died am alive again today,
and this is the sun's birthday;this is the birth
day of life and of love and of wings:and of the gay
great happening illimitably earth)

how should tasting touching hearing seeing
breathing any—lifted from the no
of all nothing—human merely being
doubt unimaginable You?

(now the ears of my ears awake and
now the eyes of my eyes are opened)

E.E. Cummings

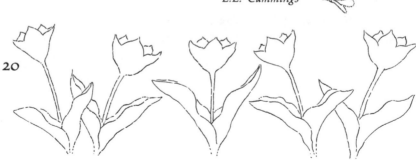

20

And God stepped out on space,
And he looked around and said:
I'm lonely—
I'll make me a world.

And far as the eye of God could see
Darkness covered everything,
Blacker than a hundred midnights
Down in a cypress swamp.

Then God smiled,
And the light broke,
And the darkness rolled up on one side,
And the light stood shining on the other,
And God said: That's good!

James Weldon Johnson
From "The Creation"

DRAWING

Lord God,
you took great big handfuls of
chaos and made galaxies
and stars and solar systems
and night and day and sun and rain and snow
and me.

I take paint and crayon and paper
and make worlds, too,
along with you.

It's fun.
Thank you.

Madeleine L'Engle

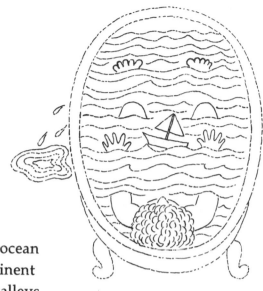

MY BATH

My bath is the ocean
and I am a continent
with hills and valleys
and earthquakes and storms.
I put the two mountain peaks of my knees
under water and bring them up again.

Our earth was like that—
great churnings and splashings,
and continents appearing and disappearing.

Only you, O God, know about it all,
and understand, and take care
of all creation.

23

Madeleine L'Engle

PIPPA'S SONG

The year's at the spring
And day's at the morn;
Morning's at seven;
The hillside's dew-pearled;
The lark's on the wing;
The snail's on the thorn:
God's in his heaven—
All's right with the world!

Robert Browning
From "Pippa Passes"

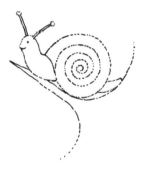

24

OUR FOOD

Lord, you have given us
all the things that grow on the earth
and all the beasts of the field and forest
for our nourishment;
and you have told us to care for them
and to tend them for you.

Help us to care for the earth, dear Lord,
and not waste or mistreat all you have given us.
Amen.

Madeleine L'Engle

25

GOD BLESS
ALL THOSE I LOVE

God bless all those I love;
God bless all those that love me;
God bless all those that love those that I love,
And all those that love those that love me.

From an old New England sampler

Lord Jesus,
help us to be more loving in our homes.
Make us thoughtful for others
and help us to think of kind things to do.
Keep us from grumbling and ill-temper
and help us to be cheerful when things go wrong
and our plans are upset.
May we learn to love
and understand each other
and think of others before ourselves.

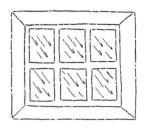

Graham Salmon

When the night is wild,
And the wind is shrewd,
God help the fishermen
Bringing me food.

When the days are cold,
And the frost is dire,
God help the miners getting
Coal for my fire.

When the winter is long,
And the earth seems dead,
God help the farmers growing
Corn for my bread.

31

Elfrida Vipont

Loving heavenly Father, who takes care of us all,
please bless all the people on the roads today:
please bless the people driving buses, cars and lorries,
please bless the people riding bicycles and scooters,
please bless the people walking and crossing busy
    roads,
please help them to be careful on the roads today
and help us to be careful when we cross the roads.

Margaret Kitson

32

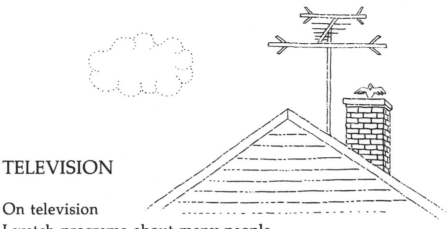

TELEVISION

On television
I watch programs about many people
from many countries.
Your people, Lord.

We are all your children
    black and white and brown and yellow,
yours.

American and Norwegian and Chinese and French
    and African and Russian and Indian and Greek
    and . . . ,
yours, dear Lord.

Thank you for being the Father
of us all. Amen.
                       33

Madeleine L'Engle

I see white and black, Lord,
I see white teeth in a black face.
I see black eyes in a white face.
Help me to see persons, Jesus—not a black person
or a white person, a red person or a yellow person,
but human persons.

Malcolm Boyd

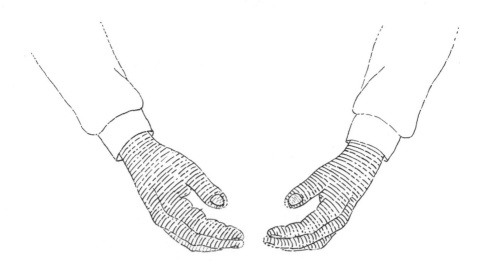

LITANY

Gather up
In the arms of your pity
The sick, the depraved,
The desperate, the tired,
All the scum
Of our weary city
Gather up
In the arms of your pity.
Gather up
In the arms of your love—
Those who expect
No love from above.

Langston Hughes

CALIBAN IN THE COAL MINES

God, we don't like to complain.
    We know that the mine is no lark.
But—there's the pools from the rain;
    But—there's the damp and the dark.

God, You don't know what it is—
    You, in Your well-lighted sky,
Watching the meteors whizz;
    Warm, with a sun always by.

God, if You had but the moon
    Stuck in Your cap for a lamp,
Even You'd tire of it soon,
    Down in the dark and the damp.

Nothing but blackness above,
    And nothing that moves but the cars. . .
God, if You wish for our love,
    Fling us a handful of stars!

Louis Untermeyer

PRAYER FOR THE PILOT

Lord of Sea and Earth and Air,
Listen to the pilot's prayer—
Send him wind that's steady and strong,
Grant that his engine sings the song
Of flawless tone, by which he knows
It shall not fail him where he goes;
Landing, gliding, in curve, half-roll—
Grant him, O Lord, a full control,
That he may learn in heights of Heaven
The rapture altitude has given,
That he shall know the joy they feel
Who ride Thy realms on birds of steel.

37

Cecil Roberts

O God, bless all the people for whom life is hard and
   difficult.
Those who are ill and who must lie in bed at home or
   in hospital;
Those who cannot walk or run or jump and play games;
Those who are lonely because they are away from
   home;
Those who are sad because someone they loved has
   died;
Those who are not very clever and for whom it is a
   struggle to keep up with the rest of the class;
Those who are shy and who find it difficult to meet
   people;
Those who are poor and never have enough.

Help me, O God, to remember all such people, and to
   do all I can to help them; through Jesus Christ my
   Lord.
Amen.

William Barclay

TINY TIM'S PRAYER

God bless us every one!

Charles Dickens
From A Christmas Carol

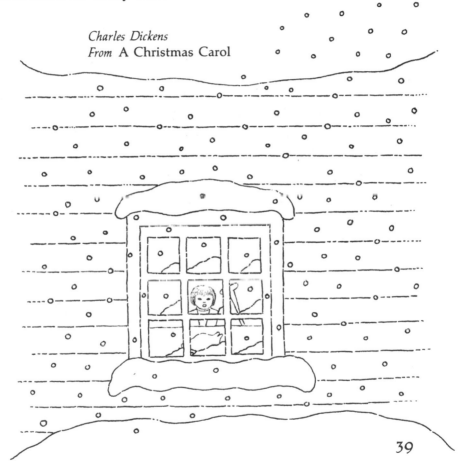

39

THE ANIMALS I LOVE

God bless the animals I love—
    Dogs wagging their tails,
    Cats and kittens purring,
    Friendly horses and ponies.

God bless the birds I love—
    Baby chickens,
    Ducks on the pond,
    Robins in the garden.

God bless all the wild creatures—
    Squirrels and hares,
    Birds building their nests,
    Larks singing.

God bless all who are kind to animals and birds
    And if people are unkind,
    Teach them to be kinder
    For Jesus' sake,
    Because he loved even the sparrows.

Elfrida Vipont

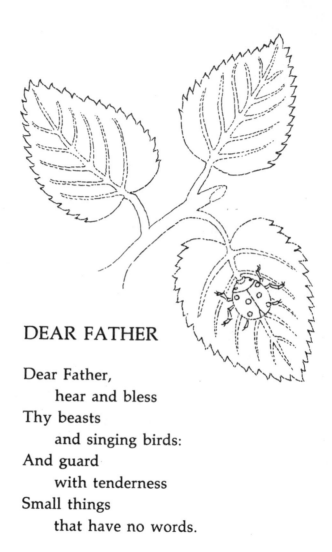

DEAR FATHER

Dear Father,
    hear and bless
Thy beasts
    and singing birds:
And guard
    with tenderness
Small things
    that have no words.

44

Author unknown

THE PRAYER OF THE LITTLE DUCKS

Dear God,
give us a flood of water.
Let it rain tomorrow and always.
Give us plenty of little slugs
and other luscious things to eat.
Protect all folk who quack
and everyone who knows how to swim.

Amen

45

Carmen Bernos de Gasztold

THE PRAYER OF THE MONKEY

Dear God,
why have You made me so ugly?
With this ridiculous face,
grimaces seem asked for!
Shall I always be
the clown of Your creation?
Oh, who will lift this melancholy from my heart?
Could You not, one day,
let someone take me seriously,
Lord?

                    Amen

Carmen Bernos de Gasztold

46

PRAYER OF THE MEXICAN CHILD

Blessed Saint George,
Safeguard your little animals,
So they won't sting
These small children.

Author unknown

47

St. George is the patron saint of all
small animals, including insects.

LITTLE THINGS

Little things, that run, and quail,
And die, in silence and despair!

Little things, that fight, and fail,
And fall, on sea, and earth, and air!

All trapped and frightened little things,
The mouse, the coney, hear our prayer!

As we forgive those done to us,
—The lamb, the linnet, and the hare—

Forgive us all our trespasses,
Little creatures, everywhere!

James Stephens

Please God, take care of little things,
The fledglings that have not their wings,
Till they are big enough to fly
And stretch their wings across the sky.

. . . .

Take care of small new lambs that bleat,
Small foals that totter on their feet,
And all small creatures ever known
Till they are strong to stand alone.

And please take care of children who
Kneel down at night to pray to you,
Oh please keep safe the little prayer
That like the big ones asks your care.

49

Eleanor Farjeon

PRAYER FOR REPTILES

God, keep all claw-denned alligators
Free.
Keep snake, and lizard, tortoise, toad,
All creep-crawl
Tip-toe turtles
Where they stand,
Keep these;
All smile-mouthed crocodiles,
Young taut-skinned, sun-wet
Creatures of the sea,
Thin, indecisive hoppers
Of the shore,

Keep these;
All hurt, haunt, hungry
Reptiles
Wandering the marge,
All land-confused
Amphibians,
Sea-driven,
Keep these;
Keep snakes, toads, lizards,
All hop, all crawl, all climb,
Keep these,
Keep these.

Patricia Hubbell

51

THE ICEBOUND SWANS

Pitiful these crying swans to-night,
caught by the ebb, or is it drought?
Without water coldly flowing at their breasts,
they, three, must die of thirst.

Without water, the firm, thin, and strong,
beating on their breasts in waves;
the great, bubbling sea all gone—
they are held on the smooth, hard, plain.

O King, who brought the tribes to liberty,
who formed heaven, who formed earth,
release, to-night, this little flock, these swans,
chastise the strong until they grow pitiful.

Author unknown
Translated from the Gaelic by Sean O'Faolain

52

BE GOOD TO ME

Dear God,
Be good to me,
The sea is so wide
And my boat is so small.

Prayer of a Breton fisherman

A CHILD'S PRAYER

Make me, dear Lord, polite and kind
 To every one, I pray.
And may I ask you how you find
 Yourself, dear Lord, to-day?

John Banister Tabb

BEDTIME

Good night.

Good night, daylight
and playing trains;
good night, books
and bread and butter,
and games of make-believe,
and brothers and sisters
and father and mother.

Good night, God.
Take care of us while we sleep,
and you have a good night, too.
Amen.

Madeleine L'Engle

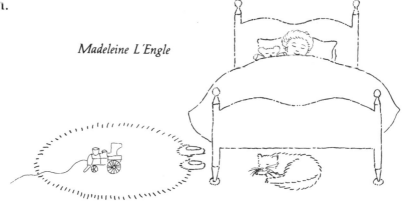

A VERSE

Father-Mother God,
    Loving me,—
Guard me when I sleep;
Guide my little feet
    Up to Thee.

Mary Baker Eddy

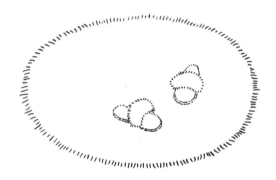

Dear God, thank you for our toys—
big ones and little ones,
old and new ones,
the ones we play with,
the ones we take to bed with us.
Help us to share our toys
with other children and to say "thank you"
to the people who gave them to us.

59

Author unknown

MORNING PRAYER

Now another day is breaking,
Sleep was sweet and so is waking,
Dear Lord, I promised you last night
Never again to sulk or fight.
Such vows are easier to keep
When a child is sound asleep.
Today, O Lord, for your dear sake,
I'll try to keep them when awake.

Ogden Nash

THOUGHTS

I want to do
What I want,
But then I find
I don't always like
What I want.
I guess, God,
You'd better
straighten me
out.

Catherine and Peter Marshall

PRAYER

Dear God,
it is often easy
to have someone do for me
the things I should do for myself.
Help me to grow strong
and self-reliant,
even if what I do
seems hard at the time.

Elizabeth McE. Shields

PLAYING

It's been a good day!

I praise you, Lord.
I praise you for a ball that bounces high.
I praise you for the friend who runs with me.
I praise you for clothes to keep me warm.
I praise you that I have been free to play
and now I'm going home.

Alleluia!

Madeleine L'Engle

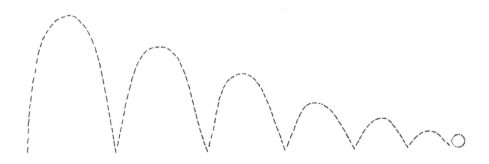

PRAYER

Dear heavenly Father,
give me the clear thinking
which will help me to do
one thing at a time,
and do it well,
for I do not want to have
a mixed-up or confused feeling
about my duties.

Elizabeth McE. Shields

64

I'VE BEEN SCOLDED

I'm sorry.
Why, Lord, is that so hard to say?

First I said: it's not my fault.
Then I said: my sister made me.
I was angry all afternoon,
with my sister, with everybody,
with myself.

Then I said: I'm sorry.
Now I'm happy with everybody,
with myself,
and with you, Lord.
Amen.

Madeleine L'Engle

PRAYER

Dear heavenly Father,
I often make mistakes
for which I do not have the courage
to take the blame.
Forgive me, God,
and help me to be so strong
that I shall never let another be blamed
for my faults, if I can help it.

66

Elizabeth McE. Shields

DIRECTIONS, PLEASE

God, help us to face up to what
We don't like
And help us prove a few things too.

When kids bug us to do a bad thing—
Tell us get out of there.

And if we don't
We hope you won't hold it
Against us,
And forgive us.

Prayer of a city kid

A CROWD

Dear God, if there's one thing
I don't need it's more people around me.
Seems like everybody is always watching me.

We need some time to think things over.
Hope you will give it to us.
And we need time to figure out what's happened.

Is it a sin, God,
To want people to leave you alone?

Prayer of a city kid

FOR SILENCE

Thank you, Lord, for silence.

The silence of great mountains and deserts and prairies.

The silence of the street, late at night, when the last travelers are safely home and the traffic is still. The silence of my room, which enables me to hear small sounds—a moth fluttering against the windowpane, the drip of dew running off the eaves of the roof, a field mouse rustling through dry leaves like an impatient clerk in search of a missing file.

Can there be complete and absolute silence?

Perhaps not. But the silence that permits small sounds to manifest themselves, small creatures to make themselves known, is a silence to be thankful for.

69

Ruskin Bond

O God, I thank you that you have made me as I am.

    I thank you for a healthy body. Help me never to
       develop habits or to indulge in pleasures which
       would make me physically less fit.
    I thank you for a healthy mind. Help me to use it
       to keep learning things, and to think until I
       reach an answer to my problems.
    I thank you for all the interest of life, that there are
       always new things to do and see.
    I thank you for the people who mean much to me
       —my friends, my teachers, my father and
       mother. Help me to live so that I will never
       disappoint them; through Jesus Christ my Lord.
       Amen.

William Barclay

God who made the earth,
The air, the sky, the sea,
Who gave the light its birth,
Careth for me.

God who made the grass,
The flower, the fruit, the tree,
The day and night to pass,
Careth for me.

God who made the sun,
The moon, the stars, is he
Who, when life's clouds come on,
Careth for me.

Sarah Betts Rhodes

71

GOD BE IN MY HEAD

God be in my head
And in my Understanding.

God be in my eyes
And in my Looking.

God be in my mouth
And in my Speaking.

God be in my heart
And in my Thinking.

God be at mine end
And at my Departing.

From a children's prayer book, 1558

LIGHT A CANDLE
WITHIN MY HEART

O thou great Chief,
light a candle within my heart
that I may see what is therein
and sweep the rubbish
from thy dwelling-place.

By an African girl

MY GIFT

What can I give Him
Poor as I am;
If I were a shepherd,
I would give Him a lamb.
If I were a wise man,
I would do my part.
But what can I give Him?
I will give my heart.

Christina G. Rossetti

76

EVENING HYMN

The day is done;
The lamps are lit;
Woods-ward the birds are flown.
Shadows draw close,—
Peace be unto this house.

The cloth is fair;
The food is set.
God's night draw near.
Quiet and love and peace
Be to this, our rest, our place.

77

Elizabeth Madox Roberts

PRAYER FOR THIS HOUSE

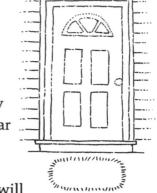

May nothing evil cross this door,
   And may ill-fortune never pry
About these windows; may the roar
   And rains go by.

Strengthened by faith, the rafters will
   Withstand the battering of the storm.
This hearth, though all the world grow chill,
   Will keep you warm.

Peace shall walk softly through these rooms,
   Touching your lips with holy wine,
Till every casual corner blooms
   Into a shrine.

Laughter shall drown the raucous shout
   And, though sheltering walls are thin,
May they be strong to keep hate out
   And hold love in.

Louis Untermeyer

HOUSE BLESSING

Bless the four corners of this house,
    And be the lintel blest;
And bless the hearth and bless the board
    And bless each place of rest;
And bless the door that opens wide
    To stranger as to kin;
And bless each crystal window-pane
    That lets the starlight in;
And bless the rooftree overhead
    And every sturdy wall.
The peace of man, the peace of God,
    The peace of Love on all!

Arthur Guiterman

79

O Great Spirit,
Whose voice I hear in the winds,
And whose breath gives life to all the world,
Hear me! I am small and weak, I need your
Strength and wisdom.

Let Me Walk In Beauty, and make my eyes
ever behold the red and purple sunset.

Make My Hands respect the things you have
made and my ears sharp to hear your voice.

Make Me Wise so that I may understand the
things you have taught my people.

Let Me Learn the Lessons you have hidden in
every leaf and rock.

I Seek Strength, not to be greater than my
brother, but to fight my greatest enemy—
myself.

American Indian prayer

Don't let my life grow dull, Lord:
I want my heart to sing
The majesty of mountains, the tint of bluebird's wing;
I want my ears to quicken
To brook-song, rhythmic, low;
When stars come out at sunset,
I want my soul to grow.
    Don't let my life grow dull!

Elizabeth McE. Shields

PRAYER

God, though this life is but a wraith,
    Although we know not what we use,
Although we grope with little faith,
    Give me the heart to fight—and lose.

Ever insurgent let me be,
    Make me more daring than devout;
From sleek contentment keep me free,
    And fill me with a buoyant doubt.

Open my eyes to visions girt
    With beauty, and with wonder lit—
But let me always see the dirt,
    And all that spawn and die in it.

Open my eyes to music; let
    Me thrill with Spring's first flutes
        and drums—
But never let me dare forget
    The bitter ballads of the slums.

From compromise and things half-done,
    Keep me, with stern and stubborn pride.
And when, at last, the fight is won,
    God, keep me still unsatisfied.

Louis Untermeyer

Give us courage, O Lord, to stand up
    and be counted,
to stand up for those who cannot stand up
    for themselves,
to stand up for ourselves when it is needful
    for us to do so.
Let us fear nothing more than we fear thee.
Let us love nothing more than we love thee, for thus
we shall fear nothing also.

Alan Paton

O Lord . . . save us
from hotheads
that would lead us
to act foolishly,
and from cold feet
that would keep us
from acting at all.

Peter Marshall

85

If only I may grow firmer, simpler—
quieter, warmer . . .

Dag Hammarskjöld

PRAYER

What shall I ask you for, God?
I have everything.
There's nothing I lack.
I ask only for one thing
And not for myself alone;
It's for many mothers, and children, and fathers—
Not just in this land, but in many lands hostile to each
    other
I'd like to ask for Peace.
Yes, it's Peace I want,
And you, you won't deny the single wish of a girl.
You created the Lord of Peace.
Where stands the City of Peace,
Where stood the Temple of Peace,
And where still there is no Peace . . .
What shall I ask you for, God? I have everything.
Peace is what I ask for,
Only Peace.

Shlomit Grossberg
Age 13

Lord, make me an instrument of thy peace;
Where there is hatred, let me sow love;
Where there is injury, pardon;
Where there is discord, union;
Where there is doubt, faith;
Where there is despair, hope;
Where there is darkness, light;
Where there is sadness, joy.

St. Francis of Assisi

SONG OF THE SKY LOOM

O our Mother the Earth, O our Father the Sky,
Your children are we, and with tired backs
We bring you the gifts you love.
Then weave for us a garment of brightness;
May the warp be the white light of morning,
May the weft be the red light of evening,
May the fringes be the falling rain,
May the border be the standing rainbow.
Thus weave for us a garment of brightness,
That we may walk fittingly where birds sing,
That we may walk fittingly where grass is green,
O our Mother the Earth, O our Father the Sky.

*From the Tewa
Indians of North America*

GOOD NIGHT

Good night! Good night!
Far flies the light;
But still God's love
Shall flame above,
Making all bright,
Good night! Good night!

Victor Hugo

YET CERTAIN AM I

I never saw a moor,
I never saw the sea;
Yet know I how the heather looks,
And what a wave must be.

I never spoke with God,
Nor visited in heaven;
Yet certain am I of the spot
As if the chart were given.

Emily Dickinson

RELIGION

I'm a believer.

I believe in kids
Who ride their bikes
Without holding on.

I believe in the chances
We take
To be complete
For one moment
With something we need.

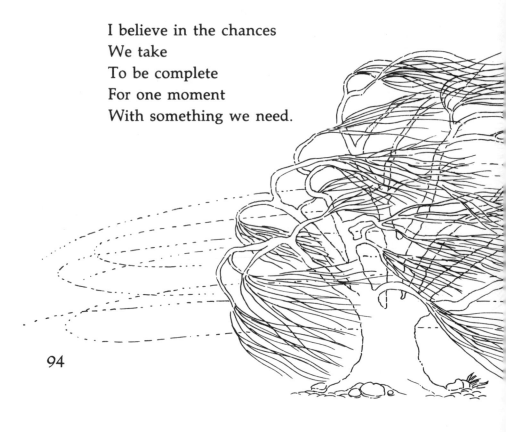

94

I believe in the crawling
And struggling
Of a baby
Much better than I believe
In his first step.

I believe in trees,
Especially willows,
That do not try to fight the wind.

And I believe in you,
Whoever you are.

I believe.

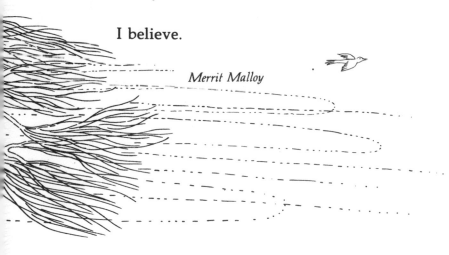

Merrit Malloy

95

My Shalom, my Peace, is hidden in every broad smile.
In every cheerful look—
My Shalom, my Peace.
It smiles at me, this Shalom of mine,
From the laughing blue eyes of a child,
From children playing in the streets.
It winks at me, my Shalom, my Peace,
And it is always around, this Shalom of mine,
Like Hope which to the heart is bound,
This Peace of mine everywhere, always will be found.

Margit Cohn
Age 15

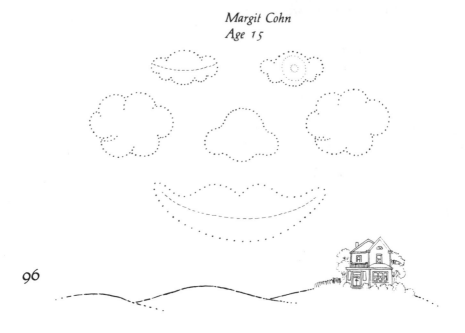

SONG FOR DOV SHAMIR

Working is another way of praying.
You plant in Israel the soul of a tree.
You plant in the desert the spirit of gardens.

Praying is another way of singing.
You plant in the tree the souls of lemons.
You plant in the gardens the spirit of roses.

Singing is another way of loving.
You plant in the lemons the spirit of your son.
You plant in the roses the soul of your daughter.

Loving is another way of living.
You plant in your daughter the spirit of Israel.
You plant in your son the soul of the desert.

Dannie Abse

PRAYER TO THE MOON

Take my face and give me yours!
Take my face, my unhappy face,
Give me your face,
with which you return
when you have died,
when you vanished from sight.
You lie down and return—
Let me reassemble you, because you have joy,
you return evermore alive,
after you have vanished from sight.
Did you not promise us once
that we too should return
and be happy after death?

From the Bushmen
Desert people of southern Africa

98

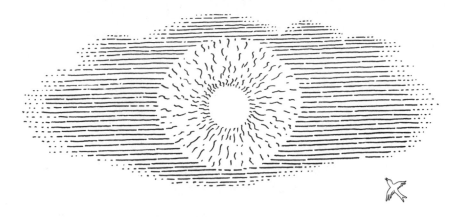

PSALM OF A BLACK MOTHER

Sometimes, I felt the sun
    didn't even shine on my street
I thought it was just for the rich
the safe,
    the other guy
And by the time it came my way
the warmth had gone away
But I found a sun
that shines even when the sky is hazy
and storm clouds roll into place
The everlasting love of Jesus
never fades
    eclipses
    or hides
It shines on all sides of my midnight world.   *99*

Theresa Greenwood

EVERY MORNING WHEN I WAKE

Every morning when I wake,
Dear Lord, a little prayer I make,
O please to keep Thy lovely eye
On all poor creatures born to die.

And every evening at sun-down
I ask a blessing on the town,
For whether we last the night or no
I'm sure is always touch-and-go.

We are not wholly bad or good
Who live our lives under Milk Wood,
And Thou, I know wilt be the first
To see our best side, not our worst.

O let us see another day!
Bless us this night, I pray,
And to the sun we all will bow
And say, good-bye—but just for now!

Dylan Thomas

TAMBOURINES

Tambourines!
Tambourines!
Tambourines!
To the glory of God!
Tambourines
To glory!

A gospel shout
And a gospel song:
Life is short
But God is long!

Tambourines!
Tambourines!
Tambourines!
To glory!

Langston Hughes

101

ACKNOWLEDGMENTS

The compiler and publisher have made every effort to trace the ownership of all material, and to the best of their knowledge have secured all necessary permissions. Should there be any correction regarding the use of any prayer or poem, the compiler, upon notification, will be pleased to make proper acknowledgment in future editions.

Sincere thanks are due to the following publishers, individuals, and agents for their cooperation in allowing the use of their material:

ATHENEUM PUBLISHERS, INC., for "White Floating Clouds," Sia chant, from James Houston, editor, *Songs of the Dream People: Chants and Images from the Indians and Eskimos of North America.* Copyright © 1972 by James Houston. A Margaret K. McElderry book (New York: Atheneum, 1972). Also for "Prayer for Reptiles" from Patricia Hubbell, *The Apple Vendor's Fair.* Copyright © 1963 by Patricia Hubbell (New York: Atheneum, 1963).

RUSKIN BOND, for "For Silence" from *To Live in Magic* by Ruskin Bond, to be published by Thomson Press, Ltd., New Delhi.

CURTIS BROWN, LTD., New York, for "Morning Prayer" from *The New Nutcracker Suite and Other Innocent Verses,* published by Little, Brown & Company, 1962. Copyright © 1961, 1962 by Ogden Nash.

CAMBRIDGE UNIVERSITY PRESS, for "Prayer to the Moon" from *African Poetry,* compiled by Ulli Beier. Published in 1966 by Cambridge University Press.

CHOSEN BOOKS, for "Night" and "Thoughts" from *God Loves You* by Catherine and Peter Marshall. Copyright © 1967 by Catherine Marshall. Published by

Chosen Books, Lincoln, Virginia 22078.

WILLIAM COLLINS SONS & CO., LTD., for "O God, bless all the people" and "O God, I thank you" from *More Prayers for Young People* by William Barclay. Published by Fount Paperbacks. Copyright 1977 by William Barclay.

CROWN PUBLISHERS, INC., for "I'm a believer" (Religion) from *My Song for Him Who Never Sang to Me* by Merrit Malloy. Copyright © 1975 by Merrit Malloy.

HARCOURT BRACE JOVANOVICH, INC., for "i thank You God for most this amazing" from *Complete Poems 1913–1962* by E.E. Cummings. Copyright 1947 by E.E. Cummings; copyright 1975 by Nancy T. Andrews. Also for "Prayer" from *The Moon and a Star* by Myra Cohn Livingston. © 1965 by Myra Cohn Livingston. Also for "Caliban in the Coal Mines" and "Prayer" by Louis Untermeyer, reprinted from his volume *Long Feud.* Copyright 1914 by Harcourt Brace Jovanovich, Inc.; copyright 1942 by Louis Untermeyer. Also for "Prayer for This House" from *This Singing World* by Louis Untermeyer, copyright 1923 by Harcourt Brace Jovanovich, Inc.; copyright 1951 by Louis Untermeyer. Also

104

for "When the night is wild" and "God bless the animals I love" from *Bless This Day,* compiled by Elfrida Vipont, © 1958 by Harcourt Brace Jovanovich, Inc.

DAVID HIGHAM ASSOCIATES LIMITED and ELEANOR FARJEON, for "Please God, take care of little things" from *Silver Sand and Snow* by Eleanor Farjeon. Published by Michael Joseph Ltd., 1951.

HODDER & STOUGHTON, LTD., for the following selections from *Prayers for Children and Young People,* edited by Nancy Martin: "Lord Jesus, help us to be more loving" by Graham Salmon; "Give us courage, O Lord" by Alan Paton; "O thou great Chief," prayer of an African girl; and "Dear God, be good to me," a prayer of the Breton fishermen. Also for "Dear God, thank you for our toys" from *Well God, Here We Are Again* by John Bryant and David Winter; © 1974 by J. A. C. Bryant and David Winter.

HOLT, RINEHART AND WINSTON, PUBLISHERS, for "I see white and black, Lord" from *Are You Running with Me, Jesus?* by Malcolm Boyd. Copyright © 1965 by Malcolm Boyd. Also for "A Prayer in Spring" from *The Poetry of Robert Frost,* edited by Edward Connery Lathem. Copyright 1934, © 1969 by Holt,

ELIZABETH McE. SHIELDS, for her poems "I often make mistakes," "It is often easy," and "Give me the clear thinking" from *As the Day Begins* (John Knox Press, 1944), and for "Don't let my life grow dull" from *In Tune with Nature's Voice* (John Knox Press, 1955).

SIMON & SCHUSTER, a Division of Gulf & Western Corporation, for "Thank You" by Lily Breek, from *The Moon Is Like a Silver Sickle,* collected and translated by Miriam Morton. Copyright © 1972 by Miriam Morton.

SMITHSONIAN INSTITUTION PRESS, for "Send Us a Rainbow" from *B.A.E. Bulletin 124, Nootka and Quileute Music* by Frances Densmore, p. 285. Smithsonian Institution, Washington, D.C., 1939. Also for "Cover my earth mother," from "Invocation to the U'wannami, Part III" in "The Zuñi Indians," translated by Matilda C. Stevenson, *B.A.E. Annual Report No. 23,* p. 176. Smithsonian Institution, Washington, D.C., 1901–1902.

VIKING PENGUIN, INC., for "The Icebound Swans," translated by Sean O'Faolin from *The Silver Branch* by Sean O'Faolin; copyright 1938 by The Viking Press, Inc., © renewed 1966 by Sean O'Faolin. Also for "The Prayer of the Little Ducks" and

"The Prayer of the Monkey" from *Prayers from the Ark* by Carmen Bernos de Gasztold, translated by Rumer Godden; English text copyright © 1962 by Rumer Godden. Also for selections from "The Creation" from *God's Trombones* by James Weldon Johnson; copyright 1927 by The Viking Press, Inc., © renewed 1955 by Grace Nail Johnson. Also for "Evening Hymn" from *Song in the Meadow* by Elizabeth Madox Roberts; copyright 1940 by Elizabeth Madox Roberts, © renewed 1968 by Ivor Roberts.

WAR RESISTERS' LEAGUE CALENDAR COMMITTEE, for "O Great Spirit" from the 1974 Peace Calendar, *As Long as the Rivers Shall Flow.*

WARNER PRESS, INC., for "Sometimes I felt the sun" from *Psalms of a Black Mother* by Theresa Greenwood. Copyright 1970, Warner Press, Anderson, Indiana.

WESTERN PUBLISHING COMPANY, INC., for "Dear Father" from *Prayers for Children.* © 1974, 1952, Western Publishing Company, Inc.

WHEELWRIGHT MUSEUM OF THE AMERICAN INDIAN, Santa Fe, New Mexico, for "Song of the Sky Loom" from *Navaho Creation Myth* by Hosteen Klah, recorded by Mary Wheelwright.

INDEXES

INDEX OF POEMS AND POETS

109

112

INDEX OF FIRST LINES

113

ABOUT NANCY LARRICK

NANCY LARRICK is well known throughout the United States and Canada for her books, magazine articles, and lectures about children and their education.

A Parent's Guide to Children's Reading, now in its fifth edition in both hardcover and paperback, was a direct outgrowth of her doctoral dissertation at New York University and won the Edison Foundation Award in 1959 as an outstanding contribution to education.

Dr. Larrick was born and grew up in Winchester, Virginia, where she now makes her home. After graduating from Goucher College, she taught in the public schools of Winchester. She was one of the founders of the International Reading Association and was second president of the organization. In 1977 she was awarded the IRA Citation of Merit and the Drexel University Citation for her contribution to children's literature.

For a number of years, Dr. Larrick was Adjunct Professor of Education at Lehigh University, where she was the director of the Poetry Workshop for Teachers. She has edited fifteen anthologies of poetry for children and young adults. The most recent of these are TAMBOURINES! TAMBOURINES TO GLORY!, a collection of children's prayers, and *When the Dark Comes Dancing,* poems for bedtime.

ABOUT GERI GREINKE

GERI GREINKE has a B.F.A. in graphics design from Philadelphia College of Art. Her illustrations have appeared in magazines, newspapers, and books; her oil paintings and lineolum block prints have been exhibited in galleries. She enjoys creating for children and teaching art to young children at St. Peter's School in Philadelphia.

117